# An *Extraordinary* Life

## One that *Counts*

by Keith Wilson

**Covenant Books UK**

COVENANT BOOKS UK (CBUK)
10 Kelsey Close, Liss. GU33 7HR
office@covenantbooksuk.org.uk
https://covenantbooksuk.org.uk/

Except where noted, scripture quotations are taken from *The Holy Bible, New International Version* (Anglicised Edition) Copyright © 1973, 1978, 1984, 2011 by Biblica (formerly International Bible Society). Used by permission of *Hodder & Stoughton Publishers*, a *Hachette UK* company. All rights are reserved worldwide. NIV® UK Trademark number 1448790. Note that occasionally, residual American spellings etc. have been corrected to English.

Photographs and diagrams are all owned by the author, except where otherwise indicated, or are in the public domain or whose use constitutes fair use under US law. Photographs from *Wikipedia* and/or *Wikimedia Commons* (https://commons.wikimedia.org/) are used under the *Creative Commons Attribution-Share Alike Unported* licence, CC BY-SA version 2.5 or higher, *Gnu* or *FDL*, or are in the public domain, unless otherwise stated.

Specifically, the cover photograph was kindly made available for reuse, and cropping, by Wikimedia user Ggia. The Renault 5 photograph was used with thanks to Wikipedia user Charles01

Created in *LibreOffice Community 24.8.1.1* with open source software on *Fedora™ 40 Linux™*.

Paperback ISBN:  9798329957273

*I dedicate this book to my wife, Cag.*

*Thank you for pointing me to Christ all those years ago by your courageous actions and words.*

*God pulled us apart and then put us back together in such a way that he would be most glorified.*

# Contents

# 1 Introduction

## Background

A question I love to ask people is: "What are your three favourite films?"

Some can answer easily by rattling off their top picks. Others might find it harder because they like so many films, and to choose three would be impossible. Some might find it hard to answer because their favourites often change according to their mood. Some people aren't especially into films so it's a bit of a non-starter.

But in my top three would be the 1989 film, *Dead Poets Society*, starring the late Robin Williams. The scene that I always enjoy watching is when the English teacher, Mr Keating, played by Robin Williams, takes his class of boys down to look at the photographs of the previous generations of students at their school, the prestigious Welton College.

He tells the boys that all of their predecessors are now fertiliser for daffodils, that is, dead. So what they must do is to make the most of their lives.

Mr Keating then gets the boys to lean into the photographs, and he whispers as if their dead predecessors were speaking to them:

*"Carpe Diem – Seize the day, boys; make your lives extraordinary!"*

This is his tactic for motivating them to grasp life and make the most of it. Knowing how much I liked this film, my wife bought me a wooden sign which hangs above my desk with those very words engraved on it:

*'Carpe diem – Seize the day'*.

So what does an extraordinary life look like? For some it might mean a life of adventure, for others a life of accomplishments. Some might see it in their affluence, others in their influence.

For some, it might be success, but for others, a life of service. Everyone wants to feel that their life matters, and no-one wants to feel as if it is being wasted.

This little book is about the extraordinary life that can be ours when we are rightly related to the God who made us.

It is not a life free of difficulties, but it is a life full of meaning.

It is not a life that guarantees success, but it is a life of joy and confidence.

It is not a life focused on leaving an earthly legacy, but a life shaped by eternity – a gift from God that we must humbly receive.

## Setting the Scene

My first car was a *Renault 5,* with the gear lever coming out of the dashboard.

It was affectionately called 'Piglet' by a friend!

One day I noticed some brown specks on both rear wheel arches. So I took some sandpaper, rubbed them off, and then resprayed with white paint. Job done!

Well not exactly, because a month or so later the same brown specks reappeared! I repeated the process. And, once again, the brown specks reappeared, as if on cue.

It was the genius, Albert Einstein, who said:

*"The definition of insanity, is doing the same things over and over again and expecting a different result."*

So, I began to poke around with a screwdriver and, to my horror, it disappeared into the side of the car leaving only the handle showing! It turned out that both wheel arches were completely rusted through; my efforts were simply masking the problem.

Although it was a shock, I needed to face up to what was really wrong before I could apply the right solution. I had to be confronted by the bad news before any good news could follow.

The same is true spiritually: We need to see the problem before we're ready and willing to hear about the solution. Jesus put it like this one day:

*"It's not the healthy who need a doctor, but the sick. I have not come to call the righteous, but sinners." (Mark 2:17)*

My aim is to introduce you to the good news of Jesus Christ and the extraordinary life that is available through him. However, the good news only makes sense if we first come face-to-face with the bad news.

To help us do this, we're dropping anchor in a short passage from the Bible. You may be familiar with the Bible, or perhaps you have never read it? It doesn't matter. Followers of Jesus believe the Bible to be God's own true revelation of himself. Through it we discover what God is like and, most importantly, how we can come to know him. The passage we're going to look at was written by a follower of Jesus, called Paul, to a group of Christians living in a city called Ephesus, part of modern-day Turkey.

Paul, or 'Saul' as he was originally called, had grown up as a very religious Jew. He then trained to become a leader within the Jewish religion. In the early days of the Christian church. Saul fiercely opposed the first Christians, and tried to get them arrested, imprisoned and executed. But one day, en route to the city of Damascus in Syria, he had an amazing encounter with

Jesus Christ which stopped him in his tracks. Jesus had died, been raised to life again, and had ascended to be with God his Father in heaven. Saul's encounter with the risen and ascended Jesus was actually the original 'Damascus Road' experience. As a result, 'Paul' as he would later be known, devoted the rest of his life to making the truth about Jesus known to others. This radical, 180-degree, 'about-turn' in Paul's life is a good reason to want to hear more about Jesus.

It was during one of Paul's later missionary journeys, in around AD 55, that he spent over two years in Ephesus telling people about Jesus Christ. Many turned and put their faith in Jesus. This was how a church came into being in that city. Paul's letter to the Ephesian church, usually called 'Ephesians', was written about five years later. At the heart of the letter is a wonderful reminder to them of the transformation that Jesus can bring about in a person's life. Here is the passage from Ephesians chapter 2:

[1] *As for you, you were dead in your transgressions and sins,* [2] *in which you used to live when you followed the ways of this world and of the ruler of the kingdom of the air* [fn 1], *the spirit who is now at work in those who are disobedient.* [3] *All of us also lived among them at one time, gratifying the cravings of our flesh and following its desires and thoughts. Like the rest, we were by nature objects of wrath.*

[4] *But because of his great love for us, God, who is rich in mercy,* [5] *made us alive with Christ even when we were dead in transgressions – it is by grace you have been saved.* [6] *And God raised us up with Christ and seated us with him in the heavenly realms in Christ Jesus,* [7] *in order that in the coming ages he might show the incomparable riches of his grace, expressed in his kindness to us in Christ Jesus.*

---

1    Usually thought to mean the devil or 'Satan'.

*⁸ For it is by grace you have been saved, through faith – and this not from yourselves, it is the gift of God – ⁹ not by works, so that no one can boast. ¹⁰ For we are God's workmanship, created in Christ Jesus to do good works, which God prepared in advance for us to do.*
*(Ephesians 2:1-10)*

We're going to look at the passage in three parts –

> The bad news (vv1-3);
>
> The good news (vv4-9);
>
> The *God* news (v10).

Then, finally, we'll think about how we should react to this news.

May I encourage you to underline the parts that interest you, put question marks next to any bits that you're not sure about, and exclamation marks next to things that shock or surprise you.

If you know someone who is a Christian, then why not ask them your questions or share with them your feelings?

Alternatively feel free to email me at:

rustywheelarches@gmail.com

and I'll try to help if I can.

# 2 The bad news

Several years ago, I attended a school reunion, meeting up with former classmates whom I hadn't seen for about 30 years. After the initial formalities were over, 'What do you do?', 'Where do you live?', 'Do you have a family?', etc., conversation then turned to, 'Do you remember when … ?' There then followed recollections of our school antics, some of which were hilarious, some acutely embarrassing, and some frankly dangerous!

Remembering what we were once like, whilst slightly uncomfortable, also served to underline the changes brought about by maturity that had, thankfully, occurred in all of our lives.

Paul begins this short section in chapter 2 of his letter by reminding his readers of what they were once like, spiritually speaking, before they came to know Jesus. If you are reading this book and would say that you don't know Jesus personally, then what Paul says in these opening verses describes you now. It doesn't make easy reading, but remember that we need to be confronted by the bad news before the good news will make any sense.

The first thing is that they were spiritually dead:

*As for you, you were dead (Ephesians 2:1)*

Paul describes here everybody's natural human state before God, and it couldn't be worse – spiritually *dead*! We are physically alive and breathing, and perhaps fit and able, but in terms of a relationship with our Creator, we are *dead*. And he tells us why; it is because of our:

*transgressions and sins (v1)*.

As soon as we hear the word *sins*, most of us automatically think of the 'bad things' that we've done – lying, stealing, cheating or hurting someone. These are certainly *sins,* but they are all symptoms of a far deeper problem: In our hearts we have all rejected God.

By nature, we don't want to have God in our lives. Of course, we might seek divine help in difficult times; after all, many people pray in a crisis. But we ourselves want to be in control of our own lives. Deep down, this is what *sin* is. It separates us from God, and makes us spiritually *dead*. Nobody naturally wants to live life God's way.

Paul then describes how we *do* naturally want to live. He describes three controlling influences that had governed the direction of the Ephesians' lives before they came to know Jesus. The first was the *world*, the second was *Satan*, and the third was their own heart-*desires*. Let's consider each of them in turn.

## The *world*

*… in which you used to live when you followed the ways of this world (v2)*

I grew up as a Marmite™ baby. I loved it, and never questioned my parents serving it up on my toast every morning, or on bread at tea time. I thought that it must be good for me or else they wouldn't give it to me. Marmite was all I knew. Only later did I realise that there was another way of life, apart from Marmite, as I discovered raspberry jam, lemon curd and then, best of all, Nutella™. If I told you that I now have a very sweet tooth you'd be unsurprised.

In describing his readers as followers of *the ways of this world,* Paul is simply describing how they lived. The *world*'s ways were all they knew (like me and

Marmite as a child). Other ways of living, especially of following God's way, were never on their radar. The original Greek word that Paul uses for the *world,* in verse 2, is 'kosmos'. This word describes the world not so much in its bigness (as we think of the 'cosmos') but in its badness. The *world* and its values are totally opposed to God and his ways. And this is true for all of us if we don't know Jesus. We may think that our lives are radical and counter-cultural, but they are still worldly and opposed to a godly mindset.

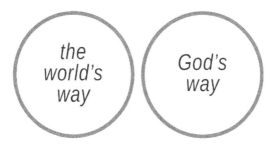

Thinking back to school maths, consider a Venn Diagram with the *world's way* and *God's way* as two 'disjoint sets', i.e. with no overlap. To follow the *world's way* is not to follow *God's way*, and vice versa.

## Satan

*… the ruler of the kingdom of the air, the spirit who is now at work in those who are disobedient. (v2)*

A couple of questions that you might have at this point are:

"Do people really believe in the existence of the devil?",

and

"Aren't followers of Satan really evil people who do terrible things (because that isn't me)?"

A little later, in the same letter to the Ephesians, Paul writes:

*'Put on the full armour of God so that you can take your stand against the devil's schemes. For our struggle is not against flesh and blood, but against the rulers, against the authorities, against the powers*

*of this dark world and against the spiritual forces of evil in the heavenly realms.' (Ephesians 6:11-12)*

This is a pretty strong warning for Paul to give if the devil doesn't exist or is merely the product of our overexcited imaginations. He sees Satan (a word in the Bible meaning 'adversary') as the same being as the *devil* (a name meaning 'accuser'). Satan is directly opposed to God and his people 24/7.

What about the notion that those who belong to Satan are really 'evil people who do terrible things'? In John's gospel in the Bible, we read of a meeting Jesus had one day with some very religious, extremely moral, Jews. They claimed to be on God's side, but were vehemently opposed to Jesus. Jesus said to them:

*"You belong to your father, the devil, and you want to carry out your father's desires." (John 8:44)*

Not believing in Jesus means not having God as our heavenly Father, but belonging instead to Satan. This doesn't equate to doing what we normally think of as 'terrible things', but it does mean that we are living in opposition to God. This may be a little hard to take, but stick with me because, as I've said, we have to understand the bad news before the good news will begin to make sense.

## Heart Desires

*All of us also lived among them at one time, gratifying the cravings of our flesh and following its desires and thoughts. (Ephesians 2:3)*

The third powerful force in our lives is simply our *desires* – the things that drive us in life. Before I came to faith in Christ three things dominated my life as a 20-something-year-old: ambition (I wanted to make lots of money), sport (I was obsessed with football), and partying (having a good time).

And your life may be focused on very different things from mine, like your family, health and fitness, holidays, your home and garden, the environment, education, keeping busy, leisure and pleasure. These are all good gifts from God that enrich our lives.

The problem is that we end up building our lives upon them like foundations, looking to them for our identity, meaning and purpose in life. Whilst we were made by God to worship him as Creator, we can end up worshipping created things instead. The focus of our hearts is not God but ourselves – it's all about me!

There's something else here that we could easily miss. We might think that Paul is some sort of religious 'goody-goody' who is pointing the finger of blame and shame at all those unbelievers out there. But look what he writes:

*All of us also lived among them at one time, gratifying the cravings of our flesh and following its desires and thoughts. (Ephesians 2:3)*

Paul lumps *us* all together, including himself. Following the world, Satan and our heart-desires is everybody's natural state.

This may not seem like an awful way to live, but it brings with it a terrible consequence. Sometimes, when children have been naughty and have deliberately disobeyed their parents, they hide when they hear their parents coming. They do this because they are afraid that their parents will do something about it, and that it probably won't be pleasant.

In doing this, they are simply following our original ancestors Adam and Eve. God had told them that they were "*free to eat from any tree*" in the Garden of Eden, but that they were not to "*eat from the tree of the knowledge of good and evil*", for if they ate from that tree, they would "*certainly die*" (Genesis 2:16-17). God had said that there would be consequences for their rebellion.

Well, Adam and Eve ate from the forbidden tree, thereby choosing to go their own way and not God's. Then we're told that they heard God walking in the garden, and they hid – just like naughty children!

But God called out to them. And after Adam and Eve had pointed the finger of blame at each other, God followed through on his warning. He tells Adam:

*"By the sweat of your brow you will eat your food until you return to the ground, since from it you were taken; for dust you are and to dust you will return."*
*(Genesis 3:19)*

Death entered the world as God's judgement for man's sin.

The terrible consequence of living in rebellion against God, following the world, Satan and our desires, is spelled out by Paul at the end of Ephesians 2:3:

*Like the rest, we were by nature deserving of wrath.*

This *wrath* is God's own hostility to sin, and his completely reasonable anger against it. It is worth noting again that Paul is not pointing the finger of judgement only at others, but including himself in this terrible position ('<u>we</u> were') .

Why does this matter? If, as some people believe, this life on earth is all that there is, then perhaps *deserving* God's *wrath* wouldn't really matter. If there were no ultimate consequences for our rebellion against God, then how we chose to live would be unimportant.

But this life is not all there is. A prophet in the Old Testament in the Bible called Daniel tells us what will take place one day:

*Multitudes who sleep in the dust of the earth will awake: some to everlasting life, others to shame and everlasting contempt. (Daniel 12:2)*

Our rebellion against God, and his reasonable anger towards sin, will result in an everlasting separation from him in hell.

But this will not be the case for everyone, because some people will be given the reality of *everlasting life* – more on this later!

In my first job in Christian ministry, I was told by someone I worked with, "just to accentuate the positive". By that he meant that people don't want to hear the bad news, so just tell them the good news.

It would be really easy to omit from this book any reference to sin, God's judgement, his anger, death or hell. After all, these are very uncomfortable truths that are hard to swallow. However, if the Christian message gets emptied of the 'bad news', the 'good news' does not have the enormous impact in our lives that it should.

I take no pleasure in laying out these difficult truths, realising that they are hard to hear and may be a shock to the system. Whilst most of us acknowledge that we're not perfect, we nevertheless hope ('fingers-crossed', 'touch wood', etc.) that God will look kindly upon us. But as we will now see, God's *kindness* is shown <u>not</u> in overlooking our sin but by tackling it head-on and personally.

# 3 The good news

Back to my
*Renault 5* car
which suffered
from rusty
wheel arches:
Once I'd got

over the shock of the screwdriver
disappearing into the bodywork, I was in a
much better position to see just how radical
the solution needed to be. It was only then
that I began to get rid of as much of the
rusty metal as I could, and apply industrial
strength car bodywork filler. It was never

'as good as new' but was certainly a huge improvement.

In the same way, with the 'bad news' of our spiritual condition clearly before our eyes, Paul then describes the radical solution that God has made available. We'll look at it in two parts – first, *what God has done* and secondly, *why God has done it*.

## What God has done

Many years ago, we were travelling through France on holiday when our car ran out of petrol. There we were by the side of a motorway, in the middle of nowhere, with no phone signal, four young children wondering what was happening, and desperate for help. We decided that my wife and three of the children would stay with the car, and that I would start walking with our older son to see if there was help to be found.

We definitely prayed, like many people do, in a panic. And amazingly, a pair of motorway workers pulled up in a van. They

helped us in ways that we weren't able
help ourselves. Without any doubt, they
rescued us. And this is the same as what
God has done for Christians – he has
rescued them, or *saved* them. We're told
this twice in the following verses from
Ephesians 2:

*… it is by grace you have been saved.
(v5, v8)*

Such a salvation is not merely from past
sins but is a permanent state of being
*saved*, for ever.

Earlier in the letter Paul states how
Christians' salvation from sin has been
accomplished. In Ephesians 1:7 he writes:

*In him* [Jesus Christ] *we have redemption
through his blood, the forgiveness of sins,
in accordance with the riches of God's
grace.*

Jesus took our *sins* upon himself on the
cross, shedding *his blood,* and dying in our
place. Three days later he rose again from
the dead. His resurrection is the proof that

his sacrifice was sufficient payment for our sin.

We are familiar with the rôle of a substitute in sport, as one player replaces another on the field of play, or in education, when a new teacher turns up because the usual one is absent. A substitute takes the place of another. The concept of substitution lies at the heart of both sin and salvation. As a Christian preacher and author once put it:

*'the essence of sin is man substituting him-self for God, while the essence of salvation is God substituting himself for man. Man asserts himself against God and puts him-self where only God deserves to be; God sacrifices himself for man and puts himself where only man deserves to be.'*
*(John Stott – The Cross of Christ)*

It would be really easy to see salvation as simply God forgiving us for our sin because Jesus pays for it instead of us. But Paul mentions three further things that God has done for us that are inseparable from our salvation and, in each case, they are also linked to Jesus Christ. First, he has:

*made us alive with Christ*
*(Ephesians 1:5);*

then he says:

*God has raised us up with Christ (v6)*

and finally, that he has:

*seated us with him in the heavenly realms in Christ Jesus. (v6)*

After Jesus died on the cross, he rose again, ascended into *heaven* where he is now *seated* at the right hand of God, his Father. Astonishingly, what Paul is saying here is that what happened to *Christ*, also happens to those who are united with him by faith. We too are *made alive*, *raised up* and *seated* in *heaven* with him.

In fact, Paul started his letter with a celebration of this exact spiritual reality:

*Praise be to the God and Father of our Lord Jesus Christ, who has blessed us in the heavenly realms with every spiritual blessing in Christ. (Ephesians 1:3)*

When we bought our first house, the place was absolutely grim, having not been decorated for thirty years or more. It was also in need of modernisation from top to bottom. What we did, though, was take lots of photos of the house in its original state, and then lots more photos once we'd done some work. These became a visual record of the gradual transformation that happened, and were a great encouragement to us.

What Paul is doing here in Ephesians is much the same thing, but he is encouraging us in terms of spiritual rather than physical transformation.

Do you remember the bad news of how Christians were spiritually dead in sin, enslaved by the world, Satan and heart-desires, subject to God's wrath and his certain judgement? But now, because of God's intervention through Jesus Christ, we are spiritually alive and seated with

Christ. We have strength to combat our own sin, and are in a relationship with God that nothing and no-one can take from us. What a transformation!

## Why God has done it

It's one thing to grasp *what* God has done, quite another to comprehend *why* God has done it. Why would God choose to save people who've rebelled against him and worshipped created things rather than him, our Creator? After the bad news of Ephesians 2:1-3 the next section begins with this:

*But because of his great love for us, God, who is rich in mercy … (Ephesians 1:4)*

This is followed by references to:

being *saved by his grace (v5, v8);*

the *incomparable riches of his grace (v7);*

and his *kindness to us in Christ Jesus (v7).*

*Love*, *mercy*, *grace*[2] and *kindness*.

It's easy to love people who love us. It's far harder to love those who don't see things the way that we do. It's virtually impossible, humanly-speaking, to love those who actively oppose us and are openly hostile. Such a seeming impossibility begins to show us something of God's *love* because, as we have seen, we are naturally his enemies and hostile to his rule. And yet we're told that God has a great *love* for us rebels (Romans 5:8), and that he is overflowing with *mercy, kindness* and *grace* towards us.

Indeed, a description of what God is like, which runs like a thread through the whole Bible, is:

*slow to anger and abounding in love*[3].

My guess is that such a description of God might come as a bit of a surprise to you?

---

2    God's undeserved favour
3    Exodus 34:6; Numbers 14:18; Nehemiah 9:17; Psalm 86:15; Psalm
      103:8; Joel 2:13; Jonah 4:2

After all, lots of people, if they imagine at all what God is like, think that he is up there watching us, just waiting for us to slip up, so that he can 'whack' us.

Years ago, when I myself was in the process of coming to faith in Christ, it was God's *love* that grabbed me. I'd been reading a story that Jesus told one day, recorded by Luke in his gospel, of a man's son who'd asked for his inheritance from his father, an act in itself that was tantamount to wishing his father dead! The father gives him his inheritance and the son goes off to a distant country and blows the lot on wild living. He ends up feeding pigs on a farm, and is so hungry that he wishes he could eat the pigs' food. For a Jewish audience, who regarded pigs as unclean animals, what Jesus describes is rock bottom.

At this point the son, we're told, *came to his senses* (Luke 15:17), and reasoned that even his father's servants were probably better off than he was. So he set off for home, willing to be a mere servant in his father's household.

Amazingly, the father was already looking out for his son. When he saw him, we're told he was:

*... filled with compassion for him; he ran to his son, threw his arms around him and kissed him. (Luke 15:20)*

Then, the father threw a big party for his son who had returned. When I read this story, I thought, 'What would I have done had I been that father, and my son had completely wasted my hard-earned wealth and brought shame on the family name?'

At the very least, I think I'd have expected a decent amount of grovelling! I'd have given him a pretty strong talking-to, and I wouldn't have wasted my much reduced resources on a party!

But, the father in the story represents God, and the way that the father treats his errant son is just the way that God responds in *love, mercy* and *kindness* to those who are his enemies. This truth 'blew me away'!

Remember that we are dead in our sins, and that dead things can't do anything to change their situation. That is why Paul writes next:

*It is by grace you have been saved, through faith – and this is not from yourselves, it is the gift of God – not by works, so that no-one can boast."*
*(Ephesians 2:8-9)*

God doesn't save us because of any actions that we may have performed, ones we think might earn his kindness towards us. Our salvation is not a reward for good behaviour or religious acts (*works*). Instead, salvation is purely a *gift* from *God*. This means that, for the Christian, there is absolutely no scope whatsoever for putting ourselves in the spotlight as if we had somehow deserved to be saved.

What we actually deserve is his anger, but what we get is his welcome! Even the faith that we exercise in putting our trust in Christ is itself a gift from God and not something that we can muster, in and of ourselves (Ephesians 2:8).

The Bible's teaching about grace[2] is a wonderful truth, but one that most people really struggle to come to terms with. After all, we live in a society built on the principle of rewarding those who work hard and keep the rules.

In the story about the son who wasted his inheritance, Jesus also tells us about an elder brother. He stayed at home with his father. He hadn't brought shame on the family name by his recklessness like the younger son, but had slaved away faithfully. He would have been a model of upright, moral, behaviour that deserved to be rewarded.

However, when his younger brother returns, and the father welcomes him and throws him a party, the elder son is furious, and refuses to join in with the party even though his father pleads with him. The elder son then tells his father this:

*"Look! All these years I've been slaving for you and never disobeyed your orders. Yet you never gave me even a young goat so I could celebrate with my friends. [30] But when this son of yours who has squandered your property with prostitutes comes home, you kill the fattened calf for him!" (Luke 15:29-30)*

The elder son cannot even bear to call the younger son his 'brother', but refers to him as '*this son of yours*'!

Lots of people read these verses and think, "He's got a point."

But here is the problem: Whom was the elder brother really trying to please – his father or himself? Did he really believe his father loved him unconditionally, or did he think he had to earn his favour by slaving away faithfully? The elder brother could not handle the concept of *grace.* That is why he exploded with rage at the *kindness, love* and *mercy* that their father had showed his brother.

Jesus told this story to a particular group of listeners:

*Now the tax collectors and sinners were all gathering round to hear him. But the Pharisees and the teachers of the law muttered,*
*"This man welcomes sinners and eats with them." (Luke 15:1-2)*

The rule-keeping and morally upright *Pharisees* and *teachers of the law* were appalled that Jesus was rubbing shoulders with scum like the '*tax collectors and sinners*'. They couldn't handle the reality of God's grace, and sincerely believed that a relationship with God was entirely down to human effort and rule-keeping.

As in Jesus' day, this mistake is all too common nowadays. But the only way that any of us can be saved by God is by realising that it only happens because of his *grace*.

As the slave trader-turned-preacher John Newton wrote in the famous hymn *Amazing Grace*:

*'Amazing Grace (how sweet the sound),*
*That saved a wretch like me!*
*I once was lost, but now am found,*
*Was blind, but now I see.'*

So, we've been confronted by the bad news: We are, by nature, spiritually dead because of sin; we are captives to the powerful influences of the world, Satan and our own desires. As a result, we deserve God's anger, and are facing his judgement.

But, the good news is that God saves people through Jesus Christ, and not because of anything they have done to deserve it, but entirely through his *grace*. He makes people spiritually alive, and seats them effectively with Christ in heaven, with power over their sin, and in a new, indestructible, relationship with himself (Romans 8:31-39).

This is all yours when you turn and put your faith in the Lord Jesus.

Finally, we come to *the God news* …

# 4 The *God* news

One of the most famous paintings in the world hangs in the Louvre art gallery in Paris: the *Mona Lisa*. Most people know that the painting was the work of Leonardo da Vinci, but very few know anything about who the woman is in the picture. I had to *Google*™ it. Apparently, she is an Italian noblewoman from the late 15th century called Lisa del Giocondo.

At the opposite end of the art spectrum, there is a small portrait of a woman, painted in October 1973, that hangs in our lounge, and is simply entitled *Grief*. The artist in this case was a less well known painter, one Gerald David Wilson, my father. No-one knows who the woman in the picture is. In her case I can't even *Google*™ it, and my father passed away  many years ago so I cannot ask him.

Why do I mention these works of art? Well, in both cases the focus tends to be on the painter, not the picture. What is invariably significant in the art world is even more important in the spiritual world.

Paul concludes the short section that we've been looking at with these words:

*We are God's workmanship, created in Christ Jesus to do good works, which God prepared in advance for us to do. (Ephesians 2:10)*

Here, the original word translated *workmanship* could also be 'masterpiece' or 'work of art'. So the person who is saved by God's grace can also be considered God's work of art!

Like paintings in a gallery, Christians put the *love, kindness, mercy* and *grace* of God on display for all the world to see. But how exactly? Paul says that it is by being:

'*created in Christ Jesus to do good works'*.

We have seen that salvation brings life where there was once death, and liberation where there was once captivity. And here, Paul writes about salvation in terms of being newly '*created in Christ Jesus'.* And where there is talk of creation taking place then there also has to be a Creator at work.

## The Creator

God's work of re-creating us *'in Christ Jesus'* is displayed before a watching world through the *'good works'* of his Christian people.

We are told that God prepared these deeds *'in advance for us to do'*. Remember that nothing we do will ever earn us salvation. It comes only through his grace. But where someone has experienced that salvation, this will be shown by *good works*. God does not present the believer with a jobs list on day one and tell them to get on with it. Rather, having been re-*created in Christ Jesus*, we will then always be getting on with the sorts of things that Jesus tells us are important.

Let's go back to the original recipients of this letter from the apostle Paul. There are six chapters in Ephesians. Broadly, the first three chapters focus on what God has done for them in Christ, as we've seen. But in the last three chapters, the focus shifts onto how these truths are to impact the lives of the believers.

Two things especially stand out; one is the *new family* that the believer joins, and the other is the *new character* that the believer displays. These are not the only changes that take place when someone begins to follow Christ, but they do give us an insight into the *'good works'* that point to God's *work* in us.

## New Family

In Ephesians chapter 4 Paul writes about the unity that followers of Jesus Christ have with each other, because they have all received the same Holy Spirit to live within them. He[4] binds them together as one people. Paul describes how Christians should be humble, gentle, patient, loving and forgiving towards one another.

In Ephesians 2:14, Paul describes how both Gentiles and Jews are now united in Jesus Christ. He explains how Christ has destroyed *'the dividing wall of hostility'*[5] between these two groups, through his death on the cross. They are now members together of God's household, brothers and sisters in Christ.

---

4    Note that God the Holy Spirit is a person, not an 'it'. See Acts 5:3; 5:32
5    This is a reference back to a wall in the temple which excluded Gentiles from Jewish worship.

Our society is chronically divided by all sorts of man-made barriers, be it race, gender, sexuality, wealth, occupation, age, education, religion and many more. But the church puts on display something radically counter-cultural: a people who are united in Jesus Christ. This is the new family that we automatically become part of from the moment we first put our trust in Jesus.

This truth hit home for me when, as a very new Christian, I was invited to Sunday lunch by a couple from the church I'd begun attending. Up until then, my Sundays had been spent playing football in the morning and then going to the pub. Now, here I was, sitting with a bunch of relative strangers, with whom I had very little in common at a human level, tucking into quiche, and drinking grape juice! But they were my brothers and sisters in Christ. And I loved it! We did not choose each other, but God chose us for each other. We were *'God's workmanship'. We* were putting his work on display!

## New Character

In Ephesians 4 and on into chapter 5, Paul describes the good character of Christians. This is to be markedly different from how they used to live before they came to faith in Christ, and different from that of people who don't follow Jesus. To help them see this, he uses the God-given metaphors of *light* and *darkness*:

*You were once darkness, but now you are light in the Lord. Live as children of light (for the fruit of light consists in all good-ness, righteousness and truth) and find out what pleases the Lord. (Ephesians 5:8-9)*

He then describes how this must impact every area of their lives: their speech, their work, their attitude to sex, their desires, their readiness to forgive others, and more.

Paul then zooms in on how following Jesus should impact their marriages, bringing up children, and doing their jobs. As these Ephesian Christians went about their ordinary lives, they were living quite differently from how they used to live. They were *God's workmanship* putting his work on display!

This is the extraordinary life that comes through faith in Christ, when we begin to follow him.

As a family, one of our favourite shops is Costco™. If you're not familiar with the chain, they have enormous warehouses which sell goods in large quantities. One big attraction for us, especially when the children were small, was all the taster stands. They allowed us to try free samples of all sorts of food and drink, obviously in the hope that we would like them so much that we'd actually buy some. On a good visit, we could get a starter, a main course, a dessert and even a drink!

As Christians, we are like those free samples, putting the *grace, love, kindness* and *mercy* of God on display for others to get a free taste. We don't draw attention to ourselves, because we have done nothing to bring about this transformation in our lives, from darkness to light. But rather, as *God's workmanship*, we are putting his work on display.

When I was in the process of coming to faith in Christ, God made use of a couple of friends in my life as two such free samples. Ed and Sarah were young twenty-somethings, like me. They were both Christians, and had dated each other for some time. We had met through work but grew in our friendship outside work too.

When I went through a painful and rather sudden relationship break-up, they were there for me, and encouraged me. They were kind, hospitable, fun to be around, but I sensed there was something else about them.

They definitely weren't 'in-your-face' about their faith, but they did speak very openly about their church. When I began to explore the Christian faith for myself, they were the first people I asked about church, and they invited me to come along too. They later gave me a Bible, introduced me to the people in their Bible study group, and encouraged me to join too.

They were free samples who put on display God's *grace, love, mercy* and *kindness,* of which I was privileged to get a taste. God used their example in order to bring about an eternal change in my life. Ed and Sarah were *God's workmanship* putting his work on display!

However, I would not want to give the impression that having this *new family* and developing a *new character* are plain-sailing, nor that we reach perfection in this life. In most of the apostle Paul's letters in the Bible to churches or individuals, he makes mention of believers who had fallen out with each other, Christians who were living more in keeping with their 'old lives' pre-Christ, rather than with their 'new lives'. Often, these were false teachers who were in danger of leading genuine believers astray.

The same problems beset Christians and churches today. Indeed, one of the criticisms that is often levelled at the church is that of hypocrisy – people saying one thing but doing another. Whilst hypocrisy is clearly not a good thing, such criticism flags up a reality about following Jesus that is often not appreciated by those who are not Christians:

Following Jesus is not a cakewalk but a conflict.

Back to the Venn Diagrams from school days: Some people think that life as a non-Christian and life as a Christian are two 'disjoint sets', i.e. that there is nothing in common. All the sins that might have plagued a person as an unbeliever are thought no longer to have any influence upon that person once they come to faith in Christ. It is imagined that you jump cleanly from one circle to the other when you become a Christian.

If this is your assumption, then of course you'll take a very dim view of anyone who professes faith in Christ and yet is not morally perfect, or of a church that makes mistakes.

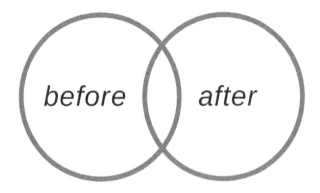

However, the reality is rather different. In practice, the 'before' and 'after' do overlap, and the Christian lives partly in the intersection – a conflict zone.

Every day Christians have to do battle with the three enemies we looked at in the first section: the world around them, Satan and their own ungodly desires.

When we are still unbelievers, although we are held captive by these enemies of God, we are not really aware of their influence upon us, or even concerned about it.

However, as soon as we put our trust in Christ, we begin to see these enemies for what they truly are. And, as with any enemy, we have to be prepared to do battle.

That is why at the end of his letter to the Ephesians, Paul devotes half of chapter 6 to the spiritual *armour* and weapons with which *God* equips the believer to engage in this battle:

*Put on the full armour of God, so that you can take your stand against the devil's schemes. (Ephesians 6:11)*

Some days we will win, and our lives will demonstrate that we are God's workmanship. But on other days, sadly, we will lose the battle, and our lives will not glorify God. This is a humbling reminder that the Christian is still a work in progress.

# 5 What will you do with the news?

In chapter 2, we were confronted by *the bad news:*

By nature we are God's enemies and in desperate need of rescue.

In chapter 3, we were encouraged by *the good news:*

God saves people through Jesus Christ, not because of anything they do to deserve it, but entirely through his grace.

In chapter 4, we were challenged by *the God news* that, as God's workmanship, Christians give the world a taste of God's *grace, kindness, love* and *mercy* that is theirs as Christians.

A remaining question is this:

What will *you* do with this news?

As you will know by now, this book is based upon a small portion of the Bible which reminds some followers of Jesus about what they were once like, and how God, through the work of his Son, transformed them. But this begs the question:

How exactly did such a change come about?

Back in Ephesians 1, Paul has already described what happened to the Ephesian Christians; this change must take place in us too:

*You also were included in Christ when you heard the message of truth, the gospel of your salvation. When you believed, you were marked in him with a seal, the promised Holy Spirit, [14] who is a deposit guaranteeing our inheritance until the redemption of those who are God's possession – to the praise of his glory. (Ephesians 1:13-14)*

One day, my wife received a text message from her sister with the news that the ballot for tickets for the *London 2012 Olympics* was closing that night. It asked us whether we had applied? As it happened, we hadn't bothered applying, because we didn't think we stood much chance of getting tickets, especially since there were six of us in the family!

Anyway, having heard this news, we acted upon it there and then, and put in an application just before the deadline. Much to our surprise, we were informed a little while later that we'd been allotted six tickets for day one of the athletics events in the Olympic stadium (which also happened to be our youngest child's birthday!) Notice how the news had to be acted upon in order for us to benefit from it.

The *gospel* (a word in the Bible meaning, simply, 'good news') of salvation is thankfully not a ballot, but it is news that must be acted upon if we are to benefit.

And that action on our part is faith:

*you believed (Ephesians 1:13)*.

Having been confronted by the bad news of our spiritual deadness, captivity to Satan, the world and our own desires, and having realised that we deserve God's anger, we must now *believe* the good news. God promises to give you new life and freedom from these enslaving powers. He does this through the death and resurrection of the Lord Jesus, and through his Holy Spirit coming to live within you.

So what must you yourself do? You must put your trust in the Lord Jesus, relying on him to take away your sins through his death on the cross. There is no special formula for how this should be done.

Some people know the exact day this took place; others would say it happened over a period of time. Some come to faith by saying a pre-written prayer, whilst others may not actually say anything at all.

Some come to faith in the company of others, perhaps at an evangelistic event, and others when no-one else is around.

Some come to faith when they're very young, and others when they're much older. The Bible contains lots of different examples of people hearing the good news of Jesus Christ and putting their trust in him. There's no set method.

In my case, I was all alone in my flat in London, sitting on the end of my bed, in the week of my 26th birthday. I had been reading through Luke's gospel over the summer, and was pondering this invitation by Jesus:

*"I say to you: Ask and it will be given to you; seek and you will find; knock and the door will be opened to you. [10] For everyone who asks receives; the one who seeks finds; and to the one who knocks, the door will be opened." (Luke 11:9-10)*

So, I took Jesus at his word, and spoke to God. I said that I was sorry for the fact that, like the younger son in the story from Luke's gospel, I'd turned my back on him and had gone my own way. I asked for forgiveness and said to God that I wanted to try to follow him.

The room didn't fill with light. Angels didn't burst out in song (in my hearing, anyway!) It wasn't a dramatic occasion in the slightest, but it was the moment I put my trust in Jesus Christ as my Saviour from sin, and as the one whom I would follow as Lord of my life.

Having read this book, perhaps you too have been confronted by the bad news, but also encouraged by the good news of what God has done for you through Jesus Christ. Why don't you speak to God, yourself, right now?

Say that you are sorry to him for going your own way, and ask him to forgive you for your sins; ask him to enable you to follow him for the rest of your life.

Don't worry too much about what and how you say it, because God knows exactly what is on your mind. He knows the desire of your heart to reach out to him. Indeed, like the father in the story I mentioned earlier who welcomed his errant son home and threw a party, God is actively waiting to embrace you and welcome you home.

In Ephesians chapter 1, Paul mentions something that God does when a person first trusts the Lord Jesus:

*When you believed, you were marked in him with a seal, the promised Holy Spirit, [14] who is a deposit guaranteeing our inheritance until the redemption of those who are God's possession – to the praise of his glory. (Ephesians 1:14)*

Back in my school days, at the start of the new year, students would be given a writing book for each subject. The first thing that everyone in the class did was to write their name clearly on the front of the book. This made it clear to the teacher and to everyone else who was the owner of the book. Similarly, God makes it clear who belongs to him, not by some external mark, but rather by coming to live in the believer by his Holy Spirit[4]. If you have ever heard the phrase 'born-again Christian', this is what is being described. This is the new birth that replaces the former spiritual deadness. By the way, all Christians are 'born again' by God's Spirit. It is not the experience of only a favoured few (John 3:7).

My first tangible experience of God's Spirit living in me as a new believer happened a few days after I'd come to faith in Christ. I had been reading Luke's gospel over the previous weeks, but it had usually felt as if it were simply words on a page. But then, one day as I left home to catch the tube to go to work, I reflected on my Bible reading earlier that morning, and how the words had really come to life! It was as if God had been speaking directly to me. I didn't know what to make of this, but it was wonderful!

Only later did I realise that this was the presence of God's Spirit living in me, the same Spirit who is the ultimate author of the Bible, as the apostle Peter writes in his second letter:

*For prophecy never had its origin in the human will, but prophets, though human, spoke from God as they were carried along by the Holy Spirit. (2 Peter 1:21)*

Not only is the *Holy Spirit* the mark of God's ownership of the believer, but Ephesians 1:14 also tells us that he is a *deposit guaranteeing* our eternal *inheritance*. If you are wealthy enough to order a new car, the dealership will probably ask for a *deposit*. If you book a holiday, the travel company will require a *deposit*. The *deposit* is not the product itself, but it is something that secures ultimate possession of that product.

The *Holy Spirit* in the lives of the believers is God's cast-iron *guarantee* that one day they will be with him in glory. The *Holy*

*Spirit* is a foretaste of the glorious future that awaits all who have turned and put their trust in the Lord Jesus.

This gives the Christian a genuine hope, not that this life will pan out perfectly, but that a bright, eternal, future awaits us beyond this life.

Paul writes of this *hope* in one of his other letters:

*May the God of hope fill you with all joy and peace as you trust in him, so that you may overflow with hope by the power of the Holy Spirit." (Romans 14:13).*

This is the extraordinary life that is available to all who turn and put their faith in the Lord Jesus Christ.

I hope you've enjoyed this little book. As I said at the start, if you've got any questions and know someone who is a Christian, then why not arrange to meet up with them. Alternatively, feel free to email me at rustywheelarches@gmail.com.

If you have turned and put your trust in the Lord Jesus, then I will be overjoyed to hear from you.

As *the God news* chapter made clear, followers of Christ become part of a new family – God's family. And his family finds its earthly expression in the local church, so it's important to begin to get involved in a church as soon as possible.

Also, if you have a friend who is a Christian, ask them if they'd be willing to read the Bible together with you. Start with one of the gospel accounts of Jesus' life, death, resurrection and ascension (Matthew, Mark, Luke or John). This is one of the best ways to become well-grounded, and to grow in your faith.

And if you haven't yet turned and put your trust in the Lord Jesus – Keep going! Keep asking God, and you will find him. Ask God to open the door and he will welcome you in (Luke 11:10).

Thanks for reading, Keith Wilson 2024

PS. You might like think about doing a <u>Christianity Explored or Hope Explored Course</u>.

# Scripture Index

## Also available on Amazon and other sellers:

**A recommended follow-up book for those who still have questions …**

Printed in Great Britain
by Amazon